JAN 2 9 2004

 W9-BGC-904

Battles of the French and Indian War

Diane Smolinski

Series Consultant:
Lieutenant Colonel G.A. LoFaro

Heinemann Library
Chicago, Illinois

Designed by Herman Adler Design
Photo research by Julie Laffin
Printed and bound in the United States by Lake Book
Manufacturing, Inc.

07 06 05 04 03
10 9 8 7 6 5 4 3 2 1

Library of Congress Cataloging-in-Publication Data
Smolinski, Diane, 1950-
   Battles of the French and Indian War / Diane
Smolinski.
      p. cm. -- (Americans at war. The French and
Indian War)
Includes bibliographical references and index.
   ISBN 1-4034-0169-1
   1. United States--History--French and Indian War,
1755-1763--Campaigns--Juvenile literature. [1. United
States--History--French and Indian War, 1755-1763--
Campaigns.] I.
Title.
   E199 S66 2002
   973.2'6--dc21
                                    2002005081

Acknowledgments
The author and publishers are grateful to the following
for permission to reproduce copyright material:
Contents page, pp. 14, 29 North Wind Picture Archives;
pp. 5, 6, 9, 12, 16, 23L, 24, 25 The Granger Collection,
New York; p. 7 The Company of Military Historians
from the book, *Military Uniforms in America: The Era of
the American Revolution 1755-1795,* plate #153; p. 8 Fort
Necessity National Historic Site; pp. 11, 22 Brown
Brothers; pp. 13, 21, 27 National Archives of Canada/
Canadian Heritage Gallery; p. 15 William L. Clements
Library, University of Michigan, Ann Arbor; pp. 17, 18,
23R Mary Evans Picture Library; p. 20 Peter Newark's
Military Pictures.

Cover photographs: (main) The Granger Collection,
New York, (border, T-B) Corbis, Sue Emerson/
Heinemann Library.

Every effort has been made to contact copyright holders
of any material reproduced in this book. Any omissions
will be rectified in subsequent printings if notice is given
to the publisher.

About the Author
Diane Smolinski is the author of two previous series of
books on the Revolutionary and Civil Wars. She earned
degrees in education from Duquesne and Slippery Rock
Universities and taught in public schools for 28 years.
Diane now writes for teachers, helping them to use
nonfiction books in their classrooms. She currently
lives in Florida with her husband, Henry, and their
cat, Pepper.

Special thanks to Gary Barr for offering comments from
a teacher's perspective.

About the Consultant
G.A. LoFaro is a lieutenant colonel in the U.S. Army
currently stationed at Fort McPherson, Georgia. After
graduating from West Point, he was commissioned in
the infantry. He has served in a variety of positions in
the 82nd Airborne Division, the Ranger Training
Brigade, and Second Infantry Division in Korea. He
has a Masters Degree in U.S. History from the
University of Michigan and is completing his Ph.D in
U.S. History at the State University of New York at
Stony Brook. He has also served six years on the West
Point faculty where he taught military history to cadets.

On the cover: This engraving shows the defeat and death of British General Edward Braddock on his march to Fort Duquesne in July 1755.
On the contents page: This print depicts the French surrender of Fort Louisbourg on July 27, 1758.

Note to the Reader
• The terms North American Indian, Indian, Indian Nation, or the specific tribe names are used here instead of Native
   American. These terms are historically accurate for the time period covered in this book.
• Casualties were not always reported during the French and Indian War. Sources sometimes state different casualties for the
   same battles or none at all. In these cases, casualty numbers in the After Action Reports simply state, "unknown."

Some words are shown in bold, **like this.**
You can find out what they mean by looking in the glossary.

Contents

Struggle for the North American Continent 4

Control of the Ohio River Territory 6

Moving Toward Fort Duquesne 8

Control of the New York Territory 10

The Battle of Lake George 12

War is Declared 13

Fort William Henry 14

The British Begin to Control the War 16

Fort Carillon 17

Fort Louisbourg 18

Fort Frontenac 19

March to Fort Duquesne 20

Invasion of Canada 21

Plains of Abraham 24

Preparing for the Final Campaign 26

Treaty of Paris 28

After the War 29

Glossary 30

Historical Fiction to Read and Places to Visit 31

Index 32

Struggle for the North American Continent

Europeans sailed to North America as early as 1494. They came to claim land for their particular country. These pioneers had to deal with the climate, the Indians, and each other.

Most North American Indians did not always welcome the Europeans. They wanted to continue living on these lands as their ancestors had done for hundreds of years. The French were mainly interested in trading with the Indians, while the British wanted to build settlements. Many Indians were friendlier toward the French, who did not want to move them from their land. During the 1700s, France and Great Britain competed for land and trade opportunities east of the Mississippi River.

Frontier Dispatch

1790 Census

Total U.S. population: 3,893,874

- Slaves: 694,207

- English and Welsh: 2,042,077

- French: 11,200

- Dutch, Scotch, Irish, German, and Hebrew made up the balance of the census population.

Europeans came to North America for new opportunities. The British settled along the east coast because the land could be easily cleared for growing crops for export to England. The ocean also provided opportunities for fishing businesses and the location was ideal for cities to develop. The French were not as interested in developing land, so they traveled further west where animals could be trapped for skins to trade. The Spanish arrived in Florida in the late 1400s and claimed territories along the southern and western parts of North America.

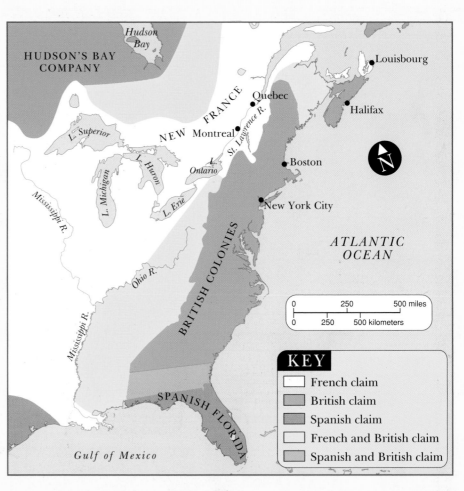

KEY
- French claim
- British claim
- Spanish claim
- French and British claim
- Spanish and British claim

Fighting on Two Continents

While the French, British, and Indians battled over land and trade rights in North America, Britain and France also fought for power in Europe. This European conflict was called the Seven Years' War.

The struggle for power in North America between France and Britain was part of this European War and was named the French and Indian War. Even though war was not declared on France in North America until May 1756, fighting between the French, Indians, British, and their **colonists** became more and more regular by 1753.

The battles discussed here were just a few of the many conflicts of the French and Indian War that were important in deciding the outcome for control of the North American continent.

George Washington, on horseback at right, was an aide to British General Edward Braddock. He gained valuable military experience during the French and Indian War.

Frontier Dispatch

Because of the great distance between North America and Europe, it took a large amount of money, many men, and the ability to coordinate their resources to fight this war.

- The distance from London, England to New York City in North America is 3,471 miles (5,586 kilometers).

- The distance from Paris, France to New York City in North America is 3,635 miles (5,850 kilometers).

Control of the Ohio River Territory

Territory Wanted by Two Countries

In October 1753, George Washington delivered a letter from the King of England to the French military commander in the **Ohio River Territory.** The letter stated that the British expected the French to leave this territory. The French commander replied that they would not be leaving.

Both Britain and France were anxious to build a fort in the wilderness land called the "Forks of the Ohio" because rivers were important for moving settlers and goods. By April 1754, the British had almost completed their fort.

At this same time, the French sailed to the Forks of the Ohio with 500 troops. When the British saw they were outnumbered, the 40 volunteers protecting the unfinished fort surrendered.

The French made the British fort larger and stronger. They named it Fort Duquesne.

The area where the Allegheny and Monongahela Rivers meet to form the Ohio River was part of the Ohio River Territory. It was referred to as the "Forks of the Ohio" at this time.

Frontier Dispatch

- The present-day city of Pittsburgh, Pennsylvania, sits on the site of Fort Duquesne.

- During the time of the French and Indian War, the Allegheny River was spelled "Alleghany."

After Action Report	British	French
Commanders	Captain William Trent	Captain Claude-Pierre de Contrecoeur
Casualties	0	0
Outcome	defeat	victory

1754	1755	1756	1757
April Surrender of the British unfinished fort			

The men in George Washington's Virginia regiment would have worn uniforms like these.

Fort Necessity

In April 1754, Colonel George Washington again left the **colony** of Virginia for the Ohio River Territory with 160 volunteers. On the way, he found out that the British had already surrendered their fort. Washington continued west to meet the French.

The French knew Washington was coming and sent men to meet him. Washington found out that the French were coming toward him and worried that they would attack. His men built a small **stockade.** Washington's men then attacked the French group by surprise and killed many of them. Washington sent the French prisoners to Virginia and requested supplies and **reinforcements.**

On June 2, 1754, Washington's Virginia **regiment** finished building the stockade and named it Fort Necessity.

Frontier Dispatch

There are many conflicting stories of what actually happened while building Fort Necessity. The French claimed that their men were only coming to talk to Washington, not to fight. The French were very angry about the killing of their men.

1758   1759   1760   1763

Moving Toward Fort Duquesne

Receiving some **reinforcements,** Washington marched 300 troops toward Fort Duquesne to try again to claim the **Ohio River Territory** for Britain. Scouts reported that a powerful French **force** was coming to meet Washington's troops. Washington decided to return to Fort Necessity.

Frontier Dispatch

This was the only time George Washington surrendered to an enemy in battle in his entire military career. Most commanders who surrender once, never get the chance to command again.

The Battle for Fort Necessity

On July 3, 1754, French forces fired from the wooded hillsides circling Fort Necessity. The pouring rain made it difficult for the British to fire their guns. By dark, nearly 100 of the 300 men inside Fort Necessity were dead or wounded. On July 4, 1754, the British surrendered and returned to Virginia. The French then burned Fort Necessity and returned to Fort Duquesne.

The French realized that the British would not stop trying to claim the land in the Ohio River Territory.

After Action Report	British	French
Commanders	Colonel George Washington	Captain Louis Coulon Ecuyer
Casualties	30 killed, 70 wounded	3 killed, unknown number of wounded
Outcome	defeat	victory

Washington and his men built Fort Necessity in a hurry. It was a small, round fort surrounded by shallow trenches. It was barely completed before the French arrived.

1754	1755	1756	1757
April Surrender of the British unfinished fort **7/4 Surrender of Fort Necessity**	**7/9 Braddock's troops attacked near Fort Duquesne**		

Another March Toward Fort Duquesne

In June 1755, British General Edward Braddock, the new commander of the British and **colonial** forces, left Fort Cumberland (now Cumberland, Maryland), with nearly 2,200 men. The British troops made slow progress because they had to build roads through forests to pull their **artillery** and supply wagons. To speed up the march, Braddock led part of his army ahead.

Stopped Again

Braddock's troops marched toward Fort Duquesne in straight, neat columns led by officers on horses. French forces and their Indian allies advanced toward the British. Once the British were close, the French and Indians hid in the forest and surrounded the British columns. They opened fire, surprising the British. British troops retreated after almost three hours of fighting. They traveled nearly 70 miles (113 kilometers) back to Fort Cumberland.

The French returned to Fort Duquesne, still in control of the Ohio River Territory.

Frontier Dispatch

General Braddock was badly wounded in this battle and died on July 13, 1755, during the retreat. His men buried him on July 14 on the path back to Fort Cumberland. All the men marched over his grave to camouflage the grave site. They did not want any Indians to find him and disturb his grave. William Shirley, governor of the Massachusetts colony and Braddock's second in command, took over after his death.

After Action Report	British	French
Commanders	General Edward Braddock	Captain Lienard de Beaujeu Contrecoeur
Casualties	more than 900 killed or wounded	23 killed, 16 wounded
Outcome	defeat	victory

As they marched toward Fort Duquesne, General Braddock's troops were attacked. Some Indians and French troops used the cover of the forest to surprise and attack their enemy.

| 1758 | 1759 | 1760 | 1763 |

Control of the New York Territory

The New York Territory stretched along the St. Lawrence River and eastern Great Lakes. The country that would control these important waterways and the surrounding land would also control the many resources of the North American wilderness.

William Shirley, the new **commander in chief** of the British **forces,** made a plan to capture Nova Scotia, Fort Niagara, and Lake George.

Nova Scotia

Throughout the 1700s, Britain and France battled over control of Nova Scotia. This land is located near the entrance to the St. Lawrence River, an important waterway connecting the Atlantic Ocean to the inside of North America.

Though war had not been declared in 1755, **colonial militia** sailed to Nova Scotia and captured two French forts. Britain now controlled the entrance to the St. Lawrence River.

The British had a fort in the New York Territory named Fort Lawrence. The French had Fort Beauséjour and Fort Gaspareau. Beauséjour was renamed Fort Cumberland by the British after they captured it.

Frontier Dispatch

William Shirley

William Shirley came to North America from England in 1731 where he spent many years in public service.

- From 1741–1756 he was the governor of the Massachusetts colony.

- In 1755, he was appointed commander in chief of British forces in North America.

- After the French and Indian War, he served as the governor of the Bahamas, another British colony.

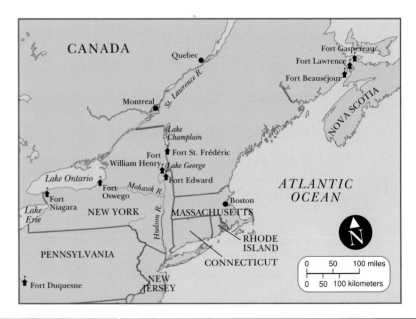

1754	1755	1756	1757
April Surrender of the British unfinished fort **7/4 Surrender of Fort Necessity**	**6/1 British capture French forts in Nova Scotia** **7/9 Braddock's troops attacked near Fort Duquesne**		

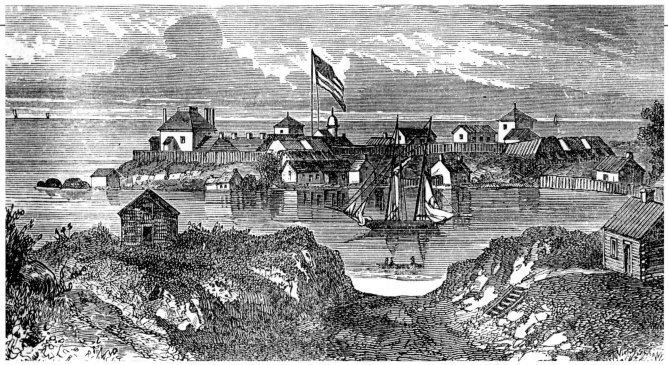

Fort Niagara stood where the Niagara River entered Lake Ontario. From this position, the fort could control access to the rest of the Great Lakes.

Fort Niagara

The British marched through the New York wilderness to capture Fort Niagara, an important French settlement on the Canadian border. On the way, they stopped at Fort Oswego. Finding it in poor condition, the army stayed to do repairs. Winter soon arrived, so the troops remained at Fort Oswego.

In August 1755, the French commander, General Dieskau, sailed from Montreal, Canada, with 3,500 troops to strengthen Fort Niagara. Leaving part of his army at Fort St. Frédéric, Dieskau led the rest toward Fort Edward, a British-held fort east of Lac St. Sacrement, or Lake George. Dieskau changed his plans and decided to go to Lake George where British troops were building Fort William Henry.

The attack of Fort Niagara would have to wait until the spring of 1756.

Frontier Dispatch

When the British reached Lac St. Sacrement, they renamed it Lake George for the British King George III. Fort William Henry was named for the son of George III.

1758   1759   1760   1763

The Battle of Lake George

The British sent troops to help defend Fort William Henry against the approaching French troops. Scouts warned the French that the British were coming. The French hid in the woods on both sides of the road, surprising and attacking the British troops. The British panicked and retreated toward Lake George.

Frontier Dispatch

Dieskau was seriously wounded and unable to retreat with his troops. He was treated at Fort Edward and eventually returned to France in 1756.

British soldiers at nearby Fort Edward heard the shots. Some came to help. Others stayed to defend the fort. French and British soldiers met on the battlefield outside of Fort Edward. The British army badly defeated the French. The French leader, General Dieskau, was wounded and the French retreated.

During the retreat, the French were attacked by another group of **colonial militia.** Many more French soldiers were killed.

The Battle of Lake George ended in a British victory.

With the help of soldiers from Fort Edward, the British troops were able to defeat the French at the Battle of Lake George.

After Action Report	British	French
Commanders	Sir William Johnson	Baron Ludwig August Dieskau
Casualties	about 189 killed or missing, about 90 wounded	about 100 killed or missing, 30 Indians killed
Outcome	victory	defeat

1754	1755	1756	1757
April Surrender of the British unfinished fort **7/4 Surrender of Fort Necessity**	**6/1 British capture French forts in Nova Scotia** **7/9 Braddock's troops attacked near Fort Duquesne** **9/8 Battle of Lake George**	**8/14 Battle for Fort Oswego**	

War is Declared

In May 1756, the British finally declared war on France.

Fort Oswego, 1756

On July 21, 1756, Louis Joseph Marquis de Montcalm left Montreal, Canada, and headed for Fort Oswego, New York, to force the British to leave the Great Lakes area. Only 1,135 British soldiers protected this unfinished fort. Montcalm approached with 3,000 men.

Star-shaped forts, like Fort Oswego, were usually made of stone and soil and often protected cities or harbors.

Battle for Fort Oswego
August 14, 1756

Montcalm first attacked Fort Ontario, a smaller fort overlooking Fort Oswego. The British realized that this French **force** was too powerful so they abandoned Fort Ontario. The French now occupied the higher ground and fired their cannons into Fort Oswego. The bombardment badly damaged Fort Oswego and killed the British commander. The British surrendered.

Montcalm promised to protect the British prisoners from Indian attack. Some Indians did not respect this promise and killed or captured many colonial and British soldiers.

After Action Report	British	French
Commanders	Colonel James F. Mercer Lt. Colonel John Littlehales (took over after Mercer was killed)	General Louis Joseph Marquis de Montcalm
Casualties	unknown	unknown
Outcome	defeat	victory

1758   **1759**   **1760**   **1763**

Fort William Henry

After the defeat at Oswego, the British worried that the French would attack their other forts in the Great Lakes area. The British hurried to finish building Fort William Henry.

Fort William Henry was positioned to protect the road from Fort Edward to Lake George. With these two forts, the British felt they better controlled the western New York Territory.

In spring 1757, British Lieutenant Colonel George Monro brought 1,500 soldiers to help strengthen the **defense** of Fort William Henry. Just 26 miles (42 kilometers) away on the north edge of Lake George, nearly 2,000 Indians in addition to 6,000 French **regulars** and Canadian **militia** met at Fort Carillon. On August 3, 1757, the French and their Indian allies sailed south on Lake George and filled the forest surrounding Fort William Henry.

During the French and Indian War, French soldiers would have had uniforms and equipment like this.

Frontier Dispatch

Indians from 33 different Indian Nations came to help the French. Some of the tribes included the Mohicans, the Iroquois, and the Huron.

1754	1755	1756	1757
April Surrender of the British unfinished fort 7/4 Surrender of Fort Necessity	6/1 British capture French forts in Nova Scotia 7/9 Braddock's troops attacked near Fort Duquesne 9/8 Battle of Lake George	8/14 Battle for Fort Oswego	8/3–9 Siege of Fort William Henry

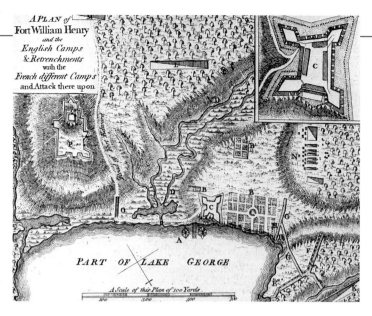

*During a **siege**, a military **force** surrounds its enemy. It keeps supplies from reaching the trapped enemy until they surrender. This is what the French did at Fort William Henry.*

The Siege of Fort William Henry
August 3–9, 1757

The French blocked the road between Fort William Henry and Fort Edward. They built **trenches,** burned buildings, and moved **artillery** and soldiers closer to Fort William Henry.

Before attacking, French General Montcalm demanded that the British surrender. Lieutenant Colonel Monro knew he could not win without **reinforcements.** No reinforcements came, so the British surrendered.

Terms of Surrender

The French agreed to lead the captured British back to Fort Edward. Again, as at Fort Oswego, the Indian allies of the French did not respect the surrender terms. They attacked and captured British soldiers and citizens. Some were able to escape to Fort Edward.

The French destroyed Fort William Henry. They badly needed supplies and were concerned about defending Canada. So, they returned to protect Fort Carillon at the north end of Lake George.

Frontier Dispatch

Some of the captured men at Fort William Henry had smallpox. The men passed it on to some Indians when they took them to their tribes. Smallpox soon spread uncontrollably through these tribes, killing many Indians.

After Action Report	British	French
Commanders	Lt. Colonel George Monro	General Louis Joseph Marquis de Montcalm
Casualties	unknown	unknown
Outcome	defeat	victory

1758   **1759**   **1760**   **1763**

The British Begin to Control the War

William Pitt, the secretary of state of England, wanted to increase British control of North America by expanding westward and conquering Canada.

Pitt sent more British soldiers to fight in North America. He also sent money for the **colonies** to pay soldiers and buy equipment and supplies. He directed the powerful British Navy to block France from sending men and supplies to North America. Pitt also appointed several new military leaders to recruit colonists, train the army, and take control of Canada.

These British leaders planned to attack four important French positions: Fort Carillon, Fort Louisbourg, Fort Frontenac, and Fort Duquesne. Once the British controlled these forts, the invasion of Canada could begin.

William Pitt was part of the British Parliament, a group of lawmakers in England. He advised the King of England on matters about the war against France.

Frontier Dispatch

The British leaders who would be heading the campaigns against the four important French forts were:

- James Abercromby—who would lead troops to Fort Carillon;

- Jeffery Amherst—who would lead troops to Fort Louisbourg;

- John Bradstreet—who would lead troops to Fort Frontenac; and

- John Forbes—who would lead troops to Fort Duquesne.

1754	1755	1756	1757
April Surrender of the British unfinished fort 7/4 Surrender of Fort Necessity	6/1 British capture French forts in Nova Scotia 7/9 Braddock's troops attacked near Fort Duquesne 9/8 Battle of Lake George	8/14 Battle for Fort Oswego	8/3–9 Siege of Fort William Henry

Fort Carillon

On July 5, 1758, a **force** of more than 16,000 British **regulars** and colonial **militia** rowed from the south shore of Lake George to Fort Carillon on the north shore. When the French saw this British force, they fled to the safety of Fort Carillon. British troops landed, set up camp, and scouted the French position. With only about 3,500 men and little food, the French prepared for the attack.

The British set up their **artillery** and began to fire. British troops formed three straight lines and marched against the French. The French **volleys** killed many British soldiers. General Abercromby misjudged the size of the French force. His larger army could have **besieged** Fort Carillon. Instead, he retreated to the south end of Lake George, defeated and embarrassed. The French did not follow. Fort Carillon and Canada remained under French control.

During battle, it was important to keep battle lines while fighting. When soldiers broke battle lines, it was often a sign of impending defeat.

Frontier Dispatch

The British sailed 800 **bateaux** and 90 whaleboats up Lake George to Fort Carillon.

After Action Report	British	French
Commanders	General James Abercromby	General Louis Joseph Marquis de Montcalm
Casualties	about 1,600	about 350
Outcome	defeat	victory

1758   **1759**   **1760**   **1763**

7/5–8 Battle at Fort Carillon

Fort Louisbourg

The British could invade Canada by sailing down the St. Lawrence River. They planned to capture Fort Louisbourg, which guarded the entrance to this important waterway.

More than 100 ships with 6,000 British troops sailed from the **colonies** to Fort Louisbourg. While British warships fired at French **shore batteries,** the British sent troops and **artillery** to the beach. General Wolfe then directed his men to take the artillery, and surround and fire on Fort Louisbourg. British warships fired on French ships until most were destroyed. The French governor of Louisbourg, Augustin Boschenry de Drucour, surrendered.

Before continuing to Quebec as planned, the British had to take 6,000 French prisoners to Europe, get new supplies for their ships, and load their **siege guns** on the ships. It was now October and too late to sail to Canada because the St. Lawrence River would soon be frozen.

Even though Fort Louisbourg was protected by harbor and fortress cannons and a rocky coastline, the British succeeded in demolishing the fort and the French ships.

After Action Report	British	French
Commanders	General Jeffery Amherst–Army	de Drucour–Army
	Admiral Edward Boscawen–Navy	des Gouttes–Navy
Casualties	7 killed, 9 wounded	2,400 seamen killed
Outcome	victory	defeat

1754	1755	1756	1757
April Surrender of the British unfinished fort **7/4 Surrender of Fort Necessity**	**6/1 British capture French forts in Nova Scotia** **7/9 Braddock's troops attacked near Fort Duquesne** **9/8 Battle of Lake George**	**8/14 Battle for Fort Oswego**	**8/3–9 Siege of Fort William Henry**

Fort Frontenac

Fort Frontenac protected the site where Lake Ontario joined the St. Lawrence River. The French stored supplies for their troops and furs to be traded in Europe there. Only 110 men protected this fort and its valuable supplies.

The British planned a secret attack. Nearly 3,000 colonial soldiers marched to the Mohawk River, boarded boats, and sailed west toward Fort Frontenac. They next crossed Lake Ontario without meeting any French ships. The British landed their boats less than a mile from Fort Frontenac. They set up **batteries** and surrounded the fort, surprising the French. The French returned fire, but surrendered within two days.

Supplies captured by the British at Fort Frontenac were badly needed by the French. By capturing Forts Louisbourg and Frontenac, the British controlled travel on the Great Lakes. General John Forbes now marched the British troops toward Fort Duquesne.

Sitting at the point where the St. Lawrence River enters Lake Ontario, Fort Frontenac could control the water route to the interior of North America.

Frontier Dispatch

Some of the supplies captured by the British at Fort Frontenac included:

- 76 cannons;
- 10,000 barrels of food, fur, and supplies; and
- 9 armed French vessels on Lake Ontario.

The supplies that were not removed were burned along with the fort.

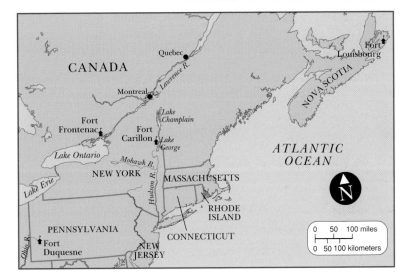

After Action Report	British	French
Commanders	Lt. Colonel John Bradstreet	Major Pierre-Jacques Payen de Noyan
Casualties	0 killed, 2 wounded	150 killed or wounded (110 regular troops, 40 Indians)
Outcome	victory	defeat

1758	1759	1760	1763

7/5–8 Battle at Fort Carillon
7/27 Battle at Fort Louisbourg
8/27 Surrender of Fort Frontenac

March to Fort Duquesne

British troops tried to keep their advance toward Fort Duquesne a secret by avoiding well-traveled roads. They often built new roads and constructed forts and blockhouses to use as supply depots along the way.

When British troops approached Fort Duquesne, they found it in ruins. During the night, the French had removed their supplies and equipment and set Fort Duquesne on fire.

Colonel Henry Bouquet, second in command of the British **forces,** stayed to build a new and much larger fort. He named this new fort, Fort Pitt. Forbes returned to Philadelphia with the rest of the troops.

The British now controlled much of the **Ohio River Territory.**

Blockhouses not only served as storage for British supplies, but they were also used during battles. Holes in the walls allowed the British to shoot at their enemies, while making it difficult for their enemies to shoot back.

Frontier Dispatch

- Fort Pitt was named in honor of William Pitt. He would be the Prime Minister of England from 1766 to 1768.

- George Washington led a Virginia **regiment** as part of the move against Fort Duquesne. After this march, he resigned from the military to marry and move to a Virginia plantation. He soon was elected to the Virginia House of Burgesses, which was the start of his political career.

After Action Report	British	French
Commanders	General John Forbes	Captain Francois-Marie Lemarchand de Lignery
Casualties	0	0
Outcome	victory	defeat

1754	1755	1756	1757
April Surrender of the British unfinished fort **7/4 Surrender of Fort Necessity**	**6/1 British capture French forts in Nova Scotia** **7/9 Braddock's troops attacked near Fort Duquesne** **9/8 Battle of Lake George**	**8/14 Battle for Fort Oswego**	**8/3–9 Siege of Fort William Henry**

Invasion of Canada

Winning many battles in 1758 helped the British to **recruit** the help of more **colonists.** The British Navy also controlled the ocean between Europe and North America. Britain was therefore able to keep its force supplied with men and equipment while keeping France from sending troops and supplies to French forces in Canada. Britain was now ready to begin its invasion of Canada.

General Jeffery Amherst now commanded the British forces in North America. General Wolfe would sail up the St. Lawrence River to Quebec and General Amherst would go across Lake Champlain or Lake Ontario to reach Montreal.

Frontier Dispatch

Jeffery Amherst was born in England in 1717. He joined the British Army at age 14 and was appointed the **commander in chief** of the British forces in North America at age 40. He remained in command of the British Army in North America until the end of the war in 1763.

The British Navy, or Royal Navy as it was also called, was larger and stronger than the French Navy during the French and Indian War. British Navy ships often prevented the French from transporting troops and supplies from France to North America.

| 1758 | 1759 | 1760 | 1763 |

7/5–8 Battle at Fort Carillon
7/27 Battle at Fort Louisbourg
8/27 Surrender of Fort Frontenac
11/25 French destroy Fort Duquesne

The St. Lawrence River near Quebec was more dangerous than in other parts. The water moved faster and the river was narrow in many places. Also, shallow waters and rocks just below the surface caused further problems for boats.

The French Prepare to Defend Quebec

Quebec, Canada sits several hundred feet above the St. Lawrence River on a high cliff.

Montcalm, a very experienced and skilled French **regular** army officer, positioned nearly 14,000 troops around Quebec. Montcalm spread his combined **force** of French regulars, Canadian **militia,** and Indian allies along the banks of the St. Lawrence River. Cannons guarded the river from key points along the cliffs, not allowing British ships to travel up the St. Lawrence. Montcalm knew that his supplies and ammunition were running low. He could not afford to let the British surround Quebec and start a **siege.**

Montcalm hoped to delay the British from attacking until winter. When the St. Lawrence froze, British ships would not be able to move supplies or **reinforcements** to help at Quebec.

Frontier Dispatch

A large British naval fleet carrying soldiers and supplies was headed down the St. Lawrence River. Captain James Cook, who would later gain fame as an explorer in the Pacific, was one of the navigators for this expedition.

The British Prepare to Attack Quebec

General Wolfe arrived in Quebec, Canada, in June 1759. When he saw the high cliffs that protected Quebec, he realized how difficult it would be to attack the city. Wolfe planned his attack carefully. He waited for General Amherst to arrive from the New York Territory. Amherst's march was delayed and he could not come to help Wolfe because winter was approaching.

Frontier Dispatch

On July 31, 1759, Wolfe did attack the French lines. Montcalm's forces held their ground. A small group of British troops then tried to climb the cliffs, but lost 440 men under heavy fire. The French only lost 60 men.

Wolfe tried to get Montcalm's soldiers to come out of their **entrenched** positions. He tried to push them back to the **fortifications** of Quebec, hoping to surround the city and start a siege. Wolfe bombarded Quebec, burned farmhouses in the surrounding countryside, and sent troops up the St. Lawrence to seize supplies and destroy French ships and ammunition. Montcalm's forces held their ground. Winter was getting closer.

James Wolfe was born into a military family. Both his father and grandfather were officers in the British Army. Wolfe's two sons also became soldiers. In 1758, Wolfe was second in command of British forces under General Jeffery Amherst.

*Louis Joseph Marquis de Montcalm joined the French Army at age fifteen. In 1756, he was sent to replace General Dieskau as the **commander in chief** of French forces in Canada.*

Plains of Abraham

By the end of August, the British General James Wolfe needed a new plan. He needed to carry out this new plan before winter.

In September, 3,600 British troops boarded boats to attack Quebec. They succeeded in getting past French lookouts. The British landed with **artillery** and supplies within two miles (three kilometers) of Quebec. A small group of men climbed a narrow path to the top of the cliffs. They captured the French guards at the top of the cliff. More soldiers climbed the cliffs. By the time Montcalm realized what was going on, Wolfe had 4,800 soldiers in battle lines on a large field near the fort called the Plains of Abraham.

With a narrow beach and sitting on a high cliff, British soldiers needed to find a way to climb the cliff to capture the city of Quebec.

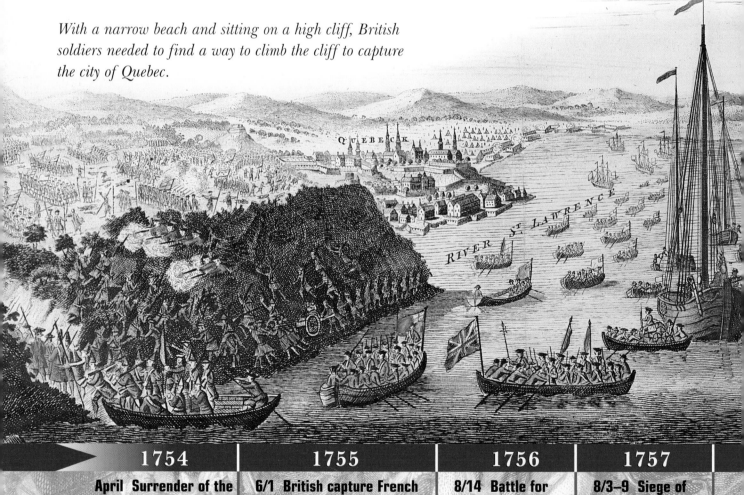

1754	1755	1756	1757
April Surrender of the British unfinished fort **7/4 Surrender of Fort Necessity**	**6/1 British capture French forts in Nova Scotia** **7/9 Braddock's troops attacked near Fort Duquesne** **9/8 Battle of Lake George**	**8/14 Battle for Fort Oswego**	**8/3–9 Siege of Fort William Henry**

Montcalm decided to drive the British troops from the Plains of Abraham before they had a chance to establish a **foothold** and take Quebec by **siege.** He ordered his army to attack. The French marched toward the battle lines of British soldiers in straight lines called ranks. The French began to fire, but the British **infantry** did not return fire until the French were very close. Once the French came within 120 feet (37 meters), the British fired their muskets into the French ranks. Montcalm rode among his soldiers on horseback trying to **rally** them, but the French army withdrew to a camp about 30 miles (48 kilometers) west of Quebec. The British captured Quebec, but did not follow the French.

With winter fast approaching, the conquest of Canada would have to wait until next year.

French and British infantry soldiers were trained to stand shoulder-to-shoulder in lines to load and fire their weapons, and then charge with their bayonets.

Frontier Dispatch

- Some British officers placed French flags on their ships. The French allowed these British boats to pass, not realizing they were British.

- Both Generals Montcalm and Wolfe died in this battle.

After Action Report	British	French
Commanders	General James Wolfe	General Louis Joseph Marquis de Montcalm
Casualties	unknown	unknown
Outcome	victory	defeat

1758	1759	1760	1763
7/5–8 Battle at Fort Carillon **7/27 Battle at Fort Louisbourg** **8/27 Surrender of Fort Frontenac** **11/25 French destroy Fort Duquesne**	**9/18 Surrender of Quebec**		

Preparing for the Final Campaign

Britain was eager to claim the rest of Canada. In the spring of 1760, the British spent several months recruiting militia and gathering supplies and equipment for the upcoming offensive against Montreal.

Finally in June, the British were ready to march to Montreal. Amherst led about 11,000 British **regulars** and **colonials** from Albany to Lake Ontario and then from the St. Lawrence River to Montreal. A second **force** of about 3,400 British regulars and colonials traveled across Lake Champlain. A third force of about 3,800 British regulars went along the St. Lawrence from Quebec to Montreal.

While these armies prepared to attack Montreal, the French decided to try to retake Quebec. Amherst sent some of his soldiers to Quebec to help defend the fort against the French attack. The British were able to turn back the French attack.

Traveling along waterways proved to be an efficient way to move an army. On boats, more soldiers with more supplies could reach places much more quickly than by foot or even by horseback.

Frontier Dispatch

By the end of 1759, Britain had control of most of North America except for Montreal and Detroit. By the end of 1760, both of these cities were under British control.

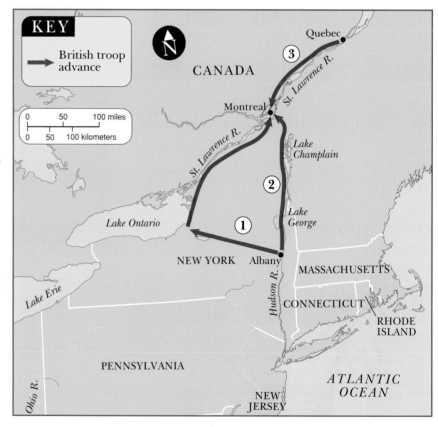

1754	1755	1756	1757
April Surrender of the British unfinished fort **7/4 Surrender of Fort Necessity**	**6/1 British capture French forts in Nova Scotia** **7/9 Braddock's troops attacked near Fort Duquesne** **9/8 Battle of Lake George**	**8/14 Battle for Fort Oswego**	**8/3–9 Siege of Fort William Henry**

With Britain now in control of the St. Lawrence River, the French at Montreal were forced to surrender because they could not get supplies to their troops.

Montreal Surrenders

In early September, British forces finally arrived outside of Montreal. On September 6, 1760, Amherst's troops crossed the river to the island of Montreal. The next day, the French asked for a peace agreement, but Amherst would only discuss surrender terms. The British continued to prepare for a **siege.** As their other two armies arrived from Quebec and Lake Champlain, the British had more than 18,000 soldiers, well-equipped and supplied. The French had only 2,100 soldiers well enough to fight, and very few provisions, cannons, or ammunition. On September 8, the surrender terms were signed. The next day, the French surrendered their **arms.** With the fall of Montreal, the British controlled all the major cities and settlements in Canada and in the North American colonies.

Smaller **skirmishes** continued for several years at French frontier forts.

After Action Report	British	French
Commanders	General Jeffery Amherst	Chevalier de Lévis
Casualties	unknown	unknown
Outcome	victory	defeat

1758	1759	1760	1763
7/5–8 Battle at Fort Carillon 7/27 Battle at Fort Louisbourg 8/27 Surrender of Fort Frontenac 11/25 French destroy Fort Duquesne	9/18 Surrender of Quebec	9/8 Surrender of Montreal	

Treaty of Paris

The Treaty of Paris was a peace agreement between Britain, France, and Spain that officially ended the French and Indian War.

The terms of the treaty gave Britain control of nearly all land in North America east of the Mississippi River, including Canada. Only the city of New Orleans became Spanish territory. The British were allowed, though, to sail the entire length of the Mississippi River. Britain also received some islands in the Caribbean Sea.

Spain received New Orleans and the territory west of the Mississippi River, called Louisiana, as a result of a previous treaty with France. They also controlled the island of Cuba.

France received two islands in the West Indies and two islands off the coast of Newfoundland, Canada. They could also fish off the banks of Newfoundland.

Once the Seven Years' War in Europe was over, a treaty called the Peace of Paris was signed by Britain, France, and Spain. It provided in great detail which islands, nations, or territories throughout the world were to be controlled by each of these countries.

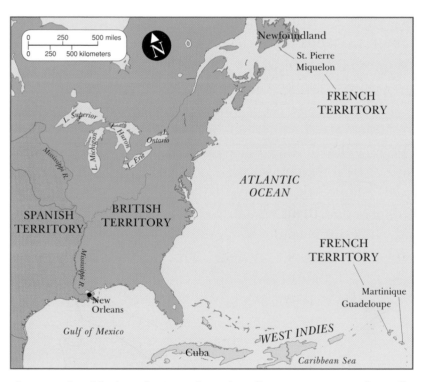

As a result of losing the French and Indian War, France lost all their territorial claims on North America east of the Mississippi River. Their claims west of the Mississippi were already handed over to Spain in 1762.

1754	1755	1756	1757
April Surrender of the British unfinished fort **7/4 Surrender of Fort Necessity**	**6/1 British capture French forts in Nova Scotia** **7/9 Braddock's troops attacked near Fort Duquesne** **9/8 Battle of Lake George**	**8/14 Battle for Fort Oswego**	**8/3–9 Siege of Fort William Henry**

After the War

Once the French and Indian War ended, **colonial** settlers traveled west across the Appalachian Mountains to hunt and farm on the frontier lands. Many Indians fought back as they felt that previous treaties they had made with the British allowed them to stay on these lands. Eventually the Indians were forced off the lands.

Events Leading to the Revolutionary War

Even though Britain now ruled the seas and controlled lands throughout the world, they were in great debt from fighting wars in North America and Europe. To pay their war debts, Britain placed additional taxes on the North American colonists. The colonists thought these taxes were unfair.

Frontier Dispatch

In an effort to prevent a war between British settlers and the North American Indians, the British government passed the Proclamation Act of 1763. This act was supposed to stop settlers from staying on lands west of the Appalachian Mountains that was marked as Indian Territory. This law was rarely enforced, as Indians were of little importance to the British after the war ended.

Beginning in 1775, the British would fight the colonists for control of North America. Colonial and British government representatives could not agree about taxes or political rights. This led to the American Revolutionary War.

The British colonies in North America now had to be concerned about fighting between the settlers moving westward and Indians.

1758	1759	1760	1763
7/5–8 Battle at Fort Carillon **7/27** Battle at Fort Louisbourg **8/27** Surrender of Fort Frontenac **11/25** French destroy Fort Duquesne	**9/18** Surrender of Quebec	**9/8** Surrender of Montreal	**2/10** Treaty of Paris

Glossary

arm   weapon

artillery   cannons

bateau   (more than one are called bateaux) small, flat-bottomed boat

battery   artillery unit of men, cannons, equipment, and horses

besiege   to surround with armed forces

blockhouse   log building with holes in the walls to shoot weapons from

colony   territory settled by people from other countries who still had loyalty to those other countries. The word *colonist* is used to describe a person who lives in a colony. The word *colonial* is used to describe things related to a colony.

commander in chief   highest ranking official in charge of all military forces

defense   protection

entrench   position dug into a hillside or area to provide shelter from gunfire and to strengthen an army's defense

foothold   position where it is difficult to move the group within it

force   group of soldiers

fortification   structure built to protect soldiers from an attacking group

infantry   foot soldiers

militia   small military unit of ordinary men organized by an individual state. Men who fought in the militia were called *militiamen*.

offensive   attack

Ohio River Territory   frontier land west of the Appalachian Mountains

pioneer   one of the first to settle in a territory

rally   to organize troops for a mission

recruit   to get someone to join the military; person who has agreed to sign up for something, usually military service

regiment   group of soldiers

regular   full-time soldier

reinforcements   troops brought to help an army under attack

secretary of state   head of a department of government

shore battery   group of cannons near the water used to protect a city or harbor

siege   capture of an opposing army by surrounding it

siege gun   cannon used to surround a city under attack

skirmish   brief fight, most often between small groups

stockade   fenced in area made of posts

supply depot   building used to store materials

trench   long, deep ditch used by the military for protection from gunfire

volley   gunfire from many weapons

Historical Fiction to Read

Keehn, Sally M. *I Am Regina*. New York: Penguin Putnam Books for Young Readers, 1991. Based on a true story about an Indian attack during the time of the French and Indian War where a ten-year-old girl is taken from her home and held by Indians from 1755–1763.

Martin, Les. *Last of the Mohicans: A Step-up Classic*. New York: Random House, 1993. A retelling of James Fenimore Cooper's original story about the friendship between a young white man and his Mohican Indian friends and the story of the conflict between the French and British.

Historical Places to Visit

Fortifications of Quebec National Historic Site
100 Saint-Louis Street
P.O. Box 2474, Main Post Office
Quebec, Quebec G1K 7R3
Canada
Visitor information: (418) 648-7016 or (800) 463-6769
Visit the site of this French and Indian War battle where the British defeated the French in 1759 at one of the last French strongholds in North America. Many bastions, gates, and defense works still stand near the city.

Fort Ticonderoga National Historical Landmark (Fort Carillon)
P.O. Box 390
Ticonderoga, New York 12883
Visitor information: (518) 585-2821
Visit the site where the French defeated a much larger British Army to maintain control of Canada during the French and Indian War. The Garrison Grounds host reenactments, fife and drum performances, and tours in both French and English.

Fort Pitt Museum (Fort Duquesne)
101 Commonwealth Place
Point State Park
Pittsburgh, Pennsylvania 15222
Visitor information: (412) 281-9284
A museum, rebuilt blockhouse, and the outline where the French and British built forts and fought over control of this important strategic position stand on this site where the Allegheny and Monongahela Rivers meet to form the Ohio River.

Fort Necessity National Battlefield
One Washington Parkway
Farmington, Pennsylvania 15437
Visitor information: (724) 329-5512
Maintained by the National Park Service, the reconstructed stockade fort built by Colonel George Washington and a small group of volunteers is part of the main section of this 900-acre national park. British General Edward Braddock's grave site and the area called Jumonville Glen, where Washington and his men surprised and killed many French, leading to the attack on Fort Necessity, are located in nearby sections of the park.

Index

Abercromby, General James 16, 17
Amherst, General Jeffery 16, 18, 21, 23, 26–27

battles
    Fort Carillon 17
    Fort Duquesne 9, 20
    Fort Frontenac 19
    Fort Louisbourg 18
    Fort Necessity 8
    Fort Oswego 13
    Fort William Henry 14–15
    in Nova Scotia 10
    Lake George 12
    Montreal 26–27
    Quebec 22–25
Bouquet, Colonel Henry 20
Braddock, General Edward 9

de Drucour, Augustin Boschenry 18
Dieskau, Baron Ludwig August 11, 12

Forbes, General John 16, 19, 20
forts
    Carillon 14, 15, 16, 17
    Cumberland 9
    Duquesne 6, 8–9, 16, 19, 20
    Edward 11, 12, 14, 15
    Frontenac 16, 19
    Louisbourg 16, 18, 19
    Necessity 7, 8
    Niagara 10, 11
    Ontario 13
    Oswego 11, 13, 15
    Pitt 20
    St. Frédéric 11
    William Henry 11, 12, 14–15

Indians 4–5, 9, 13, 14–15, 22, 29

Johnson, Sir William 12

Lake George 10–11, 12, 14
leaders, British
    Abercromby, James 16, 17
    Amherst, Jeffery 16, 18, 21, 23, 26–27
    Bouquet, Henry 20
    Braddock, Edward 9
    Forbes, John 16, 19, 20
    Johnson, William 12
    Monro, George 14–15
    Shirley, William 10
    Wolfe, James 18, 21, 23, 24–25
leaders, Colonial
    Washington, George 6, 7, 8, 20
leaders, French
    de Drucour, Augustin Boschenry 18
    Dieskau, Baron Ludwig August 11, 12
    Montcalm, Louis Joseph Marquis de 13, 15, 17, 22–23, 24–25

Monro, Lieutenant Colonel George 14–15
Montcalm, General Louis Joseph Marquis de 13, 15, 22–23, 24–25
Montreal 21, 26–27

Nova Scotia 10

Pitt, William 16, 20
Plains of Abraham 24–25

Quebec 21–23, 24–25, 26–27

Seven Years' War 5
Shirley, William 10

Treaty of Paris 28

Washington, Colonel George 6, 7, 8, 20
Wolfe, General James 18, 21, 23, 24–25